By: Latoya Dean & Aure

JASON'S ANSWERS

Illustrator: Nnanna Akwu

ISBN: 978-0692774045

Printed in the United States of America

God always answers prayer in one of three ways. It is always reassuring to know that God knows what's best for us. This book is dedicated to anyone who has ever prayed to God, and believed with all of their heart that they were heard and would receive a response. We are thankful for the vision that God so clearly gave on February 10, 2016. We honor Him for the opportunity to write the vision and make it plain. We would also like to give a special thanks to Petra, Jahni, Soraya, Jahniya, Caden, and Renate for your help with developing the vision.

We truly appreciate you.

Today was the big day. It was Prayer Sunday! Everyone came prepared for Ms. Kim's lesson about God's answers to prayer. The very first thing Ms. Kim said was, "If we ask, we shall receive, and we have not, because we ask not." Jason was super excited, because he had some big cool things he wanted to ask God for.

"Remember though, kids" Ms. Kim continued, "Even though we ask, God knows what is best for us. He answers according to His will and says yes, no, or wait."

Before Jason went to bed that night, he remembered what Ms. Kim had said about prayer, "Ask and you shall receive." Since Jason's birthday was tomorrow, he thought he would give this prayer thing a try.

Dear God,
Tomorrow is my birthday,
and I really want a green Turbo
X 3000 bicycle .... with the
yellow lightning bolts on the sides.
In Jesus name, Amen.

While Jason was sleeping,
he dreamed about receiving
that bike and believed
that he would.

The next morning Jason ran downstairs.
That's when he saw his green
Turbo X 3000 with the yellow
lightning bolts on the sides.
He yelled,
"YES! PRAYER REALLY DOES WORK!"
Yes Jason:
"How bold and free you
became in my presence, freely
asking according to my will,
sure that I was listening.
Since you were confident
that I was listening, know
that what you asked for
is as good as yours."
-1 John 5:14-15
(The Message)

That night Jason could hardly contain himself. He thought of how awesome this birthday had been, and how God had answered his prayer.

That very night Jason cooked up a new prayer. He remembered that he hadn't studied for the big spelling test all last week. He figured, if he just asked God, he could receive an A+. Jason was proud of himself.
Dear God,
I know I didn't study for the spelling test, but I know that if I ask, you will do it for me. So please, God, let me get an A+ on the spelling test.
In Jesus name, Amen.

While Jason was sleeping, he dreamed about the A+ he would receive and believed that he would.

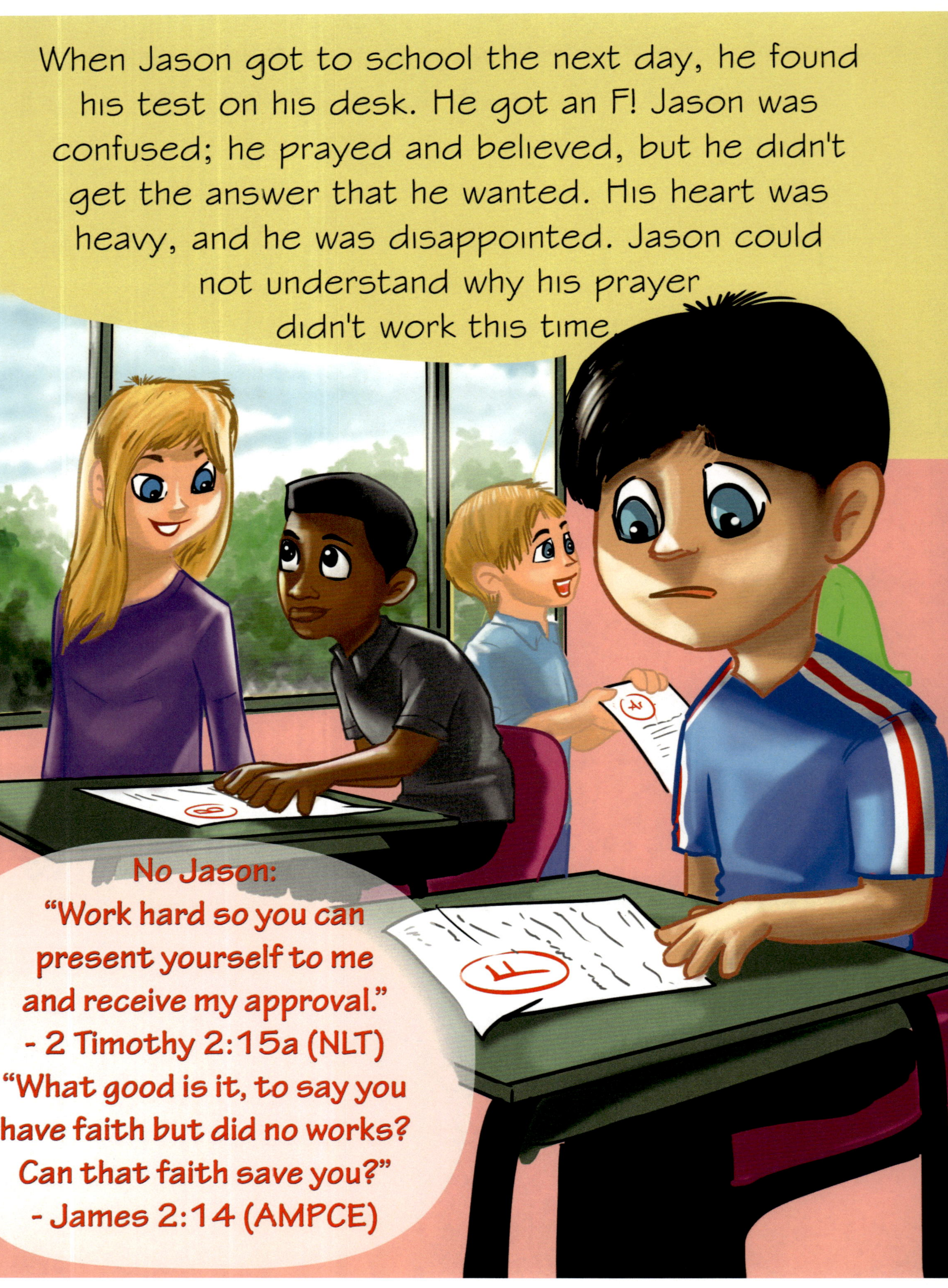
When Jason got to school the next day, he found his test on his desk. He got an F! Jason was confused; he prayed and believed, but he didn't get the answer that he wanted. His heart was heavy, and he was disappointed. Jason could not understand why his prayer didn't work this time.
No Jason:
"Work hard so you can present yourself to me and receive my approval."
- 2 Timothy 2:15a (NLT)
"What good is it, to say you have faith but did no works? Can that faith save you?"
- James 2:14 (AMPCE)
F

When Jason came home from school, he began to think. He realized that he had not studied his spelling words at all, and then it hit him! He remembered what he learned in Sunday School: "Faith without works is dead."

Jason wanted the result, but didn't put in the work. He understood now why God said no to his prayer.

That night Jason was still disappointed about the F on his test. However, he was hopeful about tomorrow's baseball practice. Jason had just made the team, and he was excited about becoming the star pitcher.
Dear God, Tomorrow is my first day at baseball practice. I really want to be the star pitcher. In Jesus name, Amen

While Jason was sleeping, he dreamed about being the star pitcher and believed that he would.

At practice the next day, Jason saw some really awesome players. He noticed Allen was a really good pitcher. Jason didn't let that stop him; he still practiced hard and was determined to be the star pitcher.

It was the day of the first game, and Coach Mark called out the starting line-up. "Pitcher ... Allen!" Jason wasn't the pitcher! He was really sad and felt like giving up.

Jason asked Coach Mark, "Why didn't you pick me to be the pitcher? I've been practicing really hard." Coach Mark replied, "Jason, you have been doing a great job. You have to keep practicing, and one day you will get your chance to pitch."

Jason practiced every chance he got.
He was determined to someday be
the star pitcher for his team.
Wait Jason:
"Wait patiently for me.
Be brave and courageous.
Yes wait patiently for me."
- Psalms 27:14 (NLT)

Some time passed, and Jason was getting better and better. He could feel himself becoming stronger. It was time for the championship game. Coach Mark called out the starting line-up, "Pitcher ... Jason!" Jason was in awe of what was happening. He finally got his chance and that day led his team to victory.

That night, as Jason thought about his day, he was overjoyed that his team won the big game. He remembered what his coach had told him, "You will get your chance." Jason thought, "Coach believed in me all along!" Even though he had to wait, Jason wouldn't change this moment for anything.

Right before bed, Jason knelt down to pray
again to God, but this time his prayer was different:
Dear God,
I am thankful for you
and all that you do in
my life. Thank you for
answering my prayers.
I know you know what
is best for me.
In Jesus name,
Amen.
For I know the plans I have for you," declares the Lord, "plans
to prosper you and not to harm you, plans to give you hope and
a future. Then you will call on me and come and pray to me, and
I will listen to you. You will seek me and find me when you seek
me with all your heart. -Jeremiah 29:11-13 (NIV)

God Answers Prayer Series

Different kids.
Different backgrounds.
Praying to the same God.

Look out for up and coming books in our God Answers Prayer Series. Jason and his friends learn more about God's love and goodness as He answers their prayers.

Contact Us:
ironsharpensironpubco@gmail.com
(954)729-8836

Made in the USA
Columbia, SC
11 May 2017